The Urgent Message

Explorer Challenge

Find out how this man
is called to the Queen ...

OXFORD
UNIVERSITY PRESS

Biff picked up a postcard in the hall. "Look," she said. "It's been written upside down and the address is wrong!"

"I'm surprised it even got here," said Chip.

"Who is it from?" asked Nadim.

"It must be from Uncle Max," guessed Chip. "He's always travelling."

"Yes, it is," said Biff. "Look! He's in Australia now."

"He's a bit of an explorer," said Mum.

"Please can I put it up in my bedroom with the others, Mum?" asked Biff.

"Of course," replied Mum.

"I collect all of his postcards," Biff explained to Nadim. "Come and see."

Nadim and Chip followed Biff upstairs to her bedroom.

4

Biff stuck the postcard to her wall with sticky tape.
She had only just finished when the key began to glow.
"Where is it going to take us now?" asked Nadim.
"Maybe to the place on Uncle Max's postcard?"

The key took them to a place that didn't look at all like the place on Uncle Max's postcard. They were in the countryside.

"Look," said Chip. He could see a building beyond the trees. "It's a castle!"

A man with a horse was standing in the middle
of the lane. He looked worried as he held one of the
horse's hooves up in the air.

"Excuse me," said Biff to the man.
"Is everything all right?"

The man looked up. "My horse needs a new horseshoe," he explained.

"Can you take it to a blacksmith?" asked Nadim.

"I don't have time," said the man. "I am a royal messenger carrying an urgent letter from King Donald. I have to take it to Queen Hilda at the castle."

"The castle isn't too far away," said Nadim. "We can deliver the letter while you go to a blacksmith."

"Really?" said the messenger. "Thank you!"

He pulled a letter from his pocket and handed it to Nadim.

The children set off towards the castle.

"Look," said Biff. "The letter has a big wax seal on it."

"That is so the person getting the letter can see no one else has read it first," said Nadim.

When they reached the castle, they told the guard that they had an urgent letter for Queen Hilda.

The guard inspected the wax seal and then said, "You'd better give this to the Queen yourselves. Follow me."

The children followed the guard into the castle
and along several dark corridors.

At last the guard stopped outside a big, wooden
door and said, "You'll find the Queen in there."

When the children opened the door,
Queen Hilda stared at them crossly.

"Why are you here?" the Queen
demanded.

Nadim held up the letter and said,
"We've brought an urgent message
for you."

The Queen took the letter but she did not open it. She glanced at the wax seal and then she cried loudly, "No, no, no! It's another letter from that awful King Donald!"

The Queen ripped up the letter and scattered the pieces on the floor.

"Aren't you even going to read it?" asked Biff. "King Donald's messenger told us it was urgent."

"You really should read it," said the royal adviser politely. "Donald *is* a king, after all."

The Queen sighed. "Very well," she said. "Give me the letter."

Two guards scrambled to collect the torn bits of paper.

The Queen held the torn pieces together and read.
Her face grew redder and redder with anger.

Dear Hilda,
I am writing to let you know that you are
very silly, in my opinion. I hope you agree.

From Donald

"How dare he call me silly!" the Queen shouted furiously.

She turned to a servant who was sitting in the corner with a quill and paper. "Write down this message at once," she said.

The servant wrote down the Queen's message: 'Dear Donald. Well, in my opinion, you are the silliest king ever! From Hilda.'

Queen Hilda smiled. "Perfect!" she said. "Now ring the bell to send for a carrier pigeon. I want the message to arrive as soon as possible."

Another servant ran
in with a pigeon.

The servant with the quill
began to attach Queen Hilda's
note to the pigeon's leg.

Nadim noticed
something on the floor.
"Hold on!" he said.
"There's another bit of
paper under the throne!"

Nadim picked up the torn pieces.

Biff still had the roll of sticky tape in her pocket and so she stuck all the pieces together.

The royal adviser looked nervous because the pigeon was about to fly off.

"Please wait!" shouted Biff. "Listen to the whole letter."

Dear Hilda,
I am writing to let you know that you are invited to my party. Our argument was very silly, in my opinion. I hope you agree.

From Donald

"How delightful!" said Queen Hilda. "Maybe
Donald isn't such a bad brother, after all."

"He's your *brother*?" asked Chip.

"Of course," replied the Queen.

"They often get cross with each other," said the
royal adviser wearily.

"Shall I let the pigeon go, Your Majesty?" asked the servant.

"No!" cried Queen Hilda. "I can't possibly send such a rude note! I must write and accept Donald's kind invitation!"

The Queen started a new letter.
"My dearest brother," she began. "How delightful to hear from you …"

As the servant scribbled down Hilda's words, the key began to glow.

"Maybe Hilda and Donald wouldn't argue so much if they didn't have to communicate by notes," said Nadim.

"Maybe," said Biff.

Kipper appeared at the door. "Come quickly!" he said. "Uncle Max is video-calling us on the computer!"

The children ran downstairs.

"Communication's much easier for us!" said Chip. "I bet Uncle Max is calling from an Internet cafe!"

But when they reached the computer, Mum and Dad looked unhappy.

"First we couldn't hear anything," said Mum.
"Then the screen froze," said Dad. "Sometimes I
think it would just be easier to use carrier pigeons!"
The children looked at each other and smiled.

Retell the Story

Look at the pictures and retell the story in your own words.

Look Back, Explorers

Why couldn't the messenger deliver the letter to Queen Hilda?

Why did the letter have a big wax seal on it?

The Queen shouted *furiously* on page 19. What other words can you think of that mean the same as *furiously*?

What might have happened if the pigeon carrying the rude note had been sent to Donald?

Can you explain what happened to the letter? Why did the meaning of the letter change in the story?

Did you find out how this man was called to the Queen?

What's Next, Explorers?

Now you know how Queen Hilda and King Donald sent messages to each other, find out about other ways people have kept in touch over time ...

Explorer Challenge
for *Smoke Signals to Smartphones*

Find out how flags help us to communicate ...